California
Becoming
a State

Elizabeth Anderson Lopez

Consultants

Kristina Jovin, M.A.T.
Alvord Unified School District
Teacher of the Year

Andrea Johnson, Ph.D.
Department of History
California State University, Dominguez Hills

Publishing Credits

Rachelle Cracchiolo, M.S.Ed., *Publisher*
Conni Medina, M.A.Ed., *Managing Editor*
Emily R. Smith, M.A.Ed., *Series Developer*
June Kikuchi, *Content Director*
Marc Pioch, M.A.Ed., and Susan Daddis, M.A.Ed., *Editors*
Courtney Roberson, *Senior Graphic Designer*

Image Credits: pp.2–3, 19, 21 (full page) North Wind Picture Archives; pp.4–5 Library of Congress [g3290.ct007271]; p.5 B Christopher/Alamy Stock Photo; pp.6–7 Sarin Images/Granger, NYC; p.7 (top) [View of Monterey Presidio, California], Malaspina Expedition drawings of California [graphic], BANC PIC 1963.002:1310-FR. Courtesy of The Bancroft Library, University of California, Berkeley; pp.8–9, 29 (top) Security Pacific National Bank Collection/Los Angeles Public Library; pp.12 (top), 31 Library of Congress [general.31218.1]; pp.12–13, 29 (bottom) Alfred Sully, Monterey, California Rancho Scene Circa 1849. Gelatin silver photograph, 8 x 10 in. The Oakland Museum of California Kahn Collection; p.14 (bottom right) Granger, NYC; p.15 Stock Montage/Getty Images; pp.16–17 DEA Picture Library/Granger, NYC; p.16 (bottom) Nicholas Philip Trist Papers, 1795-1873, Manuscript Division, Library of Congress; p.17 (bottom) Michael Freeman/Getty Images; p.18 (left) SOTK2011/Alamy Stock Photo, (right) David Rumsey Map Collection, www.davidrumsey.com; p.20 National Archives and Records Administration [558770]; p.21 (top) Niday Picture Library/Alamy Stock Photo; p.23 (bottom) Library of Congress [LC-USZ62-1286]; pp.24–25 Citizen of the Planet/Alamy Stock Photo; pp.26, 32 Courtesy of the California History Room, California State Library, Sacramento, California; p.27 Grand admission celebration. Portsmouth Square, Oct. 29th 1850, California Lettersheet Collection, courtesy, California Historical Society, Kemble Spec Col 09_B-90; p.29 (left) Dani Simmonds/Alamy Stock Photo; all other images from iStock and/or Shutterstock.

Library of Congress Cataloging-in-Publication Data
Names: Lopez, Elizabeth Anderson, author.
Title: California : becoming a state / Elizabeth Anderson Lopez.
Description: Huntington Beach, CA : Teacher Created Materials, 2018. | Includes index.
Identifiers: LCCN 2017014106 (print) | LCCN 2017017044 (ebook) | ISBN 9781425835101 (eBook) | ISBN 9781425832407 (pbk.)
Subjects: LCSH: California--History--Juvenile literature.
Classification: LCC F861.3 (ebook) | LCC F861.3 .L67 2018 (print) | DDC 979.4--dc23
LC record available at https://lccn.loc.gov/2017014106

Teacher Created Materials
5301 Oceanus Drive
Huntington Beach, CA 92649-1030
http://www.tcmpub.com
ISBN 978-1-4258-3240-7

© 2018 Teacher Created Materials, Inc.
Printed in China
Nordica.042019.CA21900332

Table of Contents

Welcome to California

California became the thirty-first state in 1850. Hundreds of years before, explorers didn't think it held much value. There seemed to be no reason to return after Juan Rodríguez Cabrillo (HWAHN roh-DREE-gehz cah-BREE-yoh) claimed the land for Spain in 1542. There was no sign of gold or silver. Ships had a hard time getting there. California was a rugged land with nothing to offer. Or so they thought.

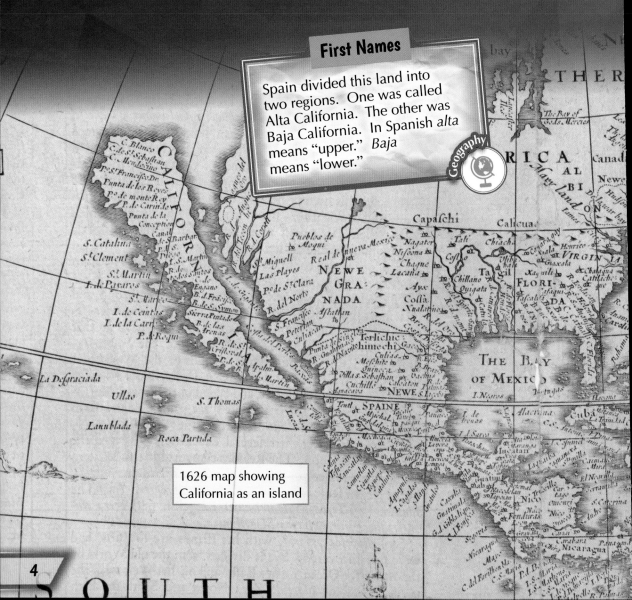

First Names

Spain divided this land into two regions. One was called Alta California. The other was Baja California. In Spanish *alta* means "upper." *Baja* means "lower."

Geography

1626 map showing California as an island

4

Spain did little with the large land along the Pacific Coast. Most of it was home to American Indians. That changed in 1769. The Spanish started to build missions there. Under the missions, only a few people had land and power. They were called **Californios**. The king of Spain gave them **land grants**. Only 30 land grants were given out, and few settlers came.

The Golden State

Early explorers thought California didn't have any gold. Hundreds of years later, they were proven wrong. In 1848, gold was found. The Gold Rush in 1849 brought many people to California.

Dual Rules

During California's early years, Spain and Mexico ruled the region. Spain was first to claim the land.

Starting in 1769, Spanish leaders **governed** the land through the use of churches and guns. They built missions in Alta California. The priests **converted** the native people to Christianity. The priests forced them to learn new skills and to adopt a new way of life.

Spain's army played a big role in the region, too. Spain's land was split into four parts. Each part had an army fort called a *presidio*. The soldiers in these forts watched over the missions and the land. The army worked with the priests. They enforced the rules of the land.

New Diseases to California

The Spanish brought problems to the area. They brought diseases, such as the flu and measles. Many American Indians became sick and died.

Presidio of San Francisco

Presidio of Monterey

Historic Events Coast to Coast

In 1776, Spanish settlers came to the West Coast. They wanted to colonize the bay area. This area would later be named San Francisco. It was an important year on the East Coast, too. Members of Congress signed the Declaration of Independence. The colonies were breaking away from Great Britain's rule.

Civics

Mapmakers

Ranchers needed a way to mark ownership of their properties. They used drawings called *diseños* (dih-SEHN-yohs). These were hand-drawn maps. Diseños showed boundaries and landmarks.

S 32 P.

Mexican Rule

In 1821, Mexico won its freedom from Spain. Alta California was now part of Mexico. Many things began to change.

The biggest change had to do with who owned the land. Under Mexico's rule, it was much easier to get land. Mexican leaders gave land grants called **ranchos** starting in 1834. Hundreds of land grants were given over the next 12 years. These years are known as the *rancho period*.

The missions changed, too. Mexico wanted to secularize them. This meant the church would no longer be in control of them. The government would run them.

The changes in power and land opened the door for new people to come. American trappers began to arrive. They trapped animals and made money by selling furs.

Rancho San Pedro

Rancho San Pedro (shown here) was the site of the first land grant given by the Spanish government. In 1784, the king of Spain gave it to Juan José Domínguez. Even when Mexico gained its independence in 1821, the land stayed in the family. Since then, it has been passed down to other family members. It remains in the Domínguez family today.

Civics

Setting the Stage for Conflict

The change in the mission system meant priests no longer held all the power. The power shifted to the ranchers. They could now own the land that once belonged to the missions. It made them rich and powerful. The ranchers became the new leaders. The ranchers mostly lived on large ranchos located in the south.

Monterey was the capital of Alta California for both Spain and Mexico. Ranchers wanted to move the capital to Los Angeles. Traders wanted the capital to stay in Monterey. More and more traders had settled in the north. The capital was a place of power. Traders and ranchers both wanted the power. They each had a different vision for the future of the land they shared.

One Capital, Five Cities

Since 1849, California has had five capitals. After Monterey, there was San Jose, Vallejo, and Benicia. In 1854, the capital was moved to Sacramento where it has stayed ever since.

Geography

State Capitol

California's capitol building is based on the one in Washington, DC. In the 1970s, the state's building was **restored**. Experts were scared that it would fall apart in an earthquake. It took six years to complete the restoration.

state capitol building

Freedom for All

In 1824, the Mexican leaders passed a law. It **barred** the buying or the selling of people to work. This law also said children of enslaved people must be freed when they turned 14. The law meant that any enslaved person who came to the area would be freed.

Civics

CONSTITUCION FEDERAL

DE LOS ESTADOS UNIDOS
MEXICANOS.

Sancionada por el Congreso General Constituyente, el 4. de Octubre de
1824.

Imprenta del Supremo Gobierno de los Estados-
unidos mexicanos, en Palacio.

The first Mexican Constitution was written in 1824.

California rancho

People on the Move

Life for the ranchers improved under Mexican rule. But life did not improve for American Indians. They **abided** by the rules of the Spanish priests. Now, they worked for the ranchers for little food and poor shelter. The American Indians were legally free, but they were trapped in this new system.

In 1824, the Mexican government passed a law. The law allowed foreign people to get land. Most people who came for the land were Americans. They had to do two things before they could get the land. First, they had to become Mexican citizens. Second, they had to convert to the Catholic religion. Most settlers did both things and got their land. But many never gave up their American roots. It wouldn't be long before the United States would be in charge of this area.

John Sutter

One of the early immigrants to this region was John Sutter. He was given land along the Sacramento River. Years later, gold would be discovered on his land.

War with Mexico

The United States and Mexico did not agree on many issues. Things got worse in 1845. Mexico warned the United States not to **annex** Texas. But the United States did not listen. The two countries were on the verge of war.

Raising the Flag

The Mexican-American War began in April 1846. One of the early conflicts took place in California. In June, a band of U.S. settlers **revolted** and seized the city of Sonoma. They claimed it to be free from Mexican rule. Several local leaders were taken as prisoners. All this was done without guns.

The Americans raised a flag. It had a star and a bear on it. The words "California Republic" were on the flag, too. This battle became known as the *Bear Flag Revolt*. The bear flag stayed up for one month. In July, the U.S. flag took its place.

Different Times, Similar Flags

Today, the California state flag (shown left) is very similar to the flag raised during the Bear Flag Revolt. Both flags have a bear, a star, and the words "California Republic."

John Frémont was an American army officer. He came to California in the spring of 1846. No one is sure if he was ordered to start a revolt. But he did. Frémont urged American settlers to form a militia and rebel against Mexico. He inspired the Bear Flag Revolt.

Frémont holds the flag marking California's independence.

The Mexican-American War

In 1846, California was still a part of Mexico. Mexican troops attacked American soldiers in Texas. The war went on for two years. In that time, U.S. troops never lost a major battle. In the end, the United States won the war.

Each side paid a high price for the war. More than 13,000 Americans died. Diseases and soiled living conditions claimed most lives. For every one man killed in battle, seven men died from illnesses. Mexico's death toll was even higher. It lost twice as many people.

At the end of the war, the two countries signed a **treaty**. This deal let the United States buy a huge piece of land. The land was in the West. That was how California became part of the United States. It was 1848, and the country was changed forever.

The Treaty of Guadalupe Hidalgo was signed at the end of the war.

Amphibious Assault

General Winfield Scott led the first attack on Mexico from the sea. Surfboats carried 10,000 men ashore. The people in Vera Cruz did not put up a fight. This landing was the largest by sea for U.S. forces. It would remain the largest until World War II.

American ships attack Mexico.

First Photos

This was the first war to be photographed. People used a new form of photography called **daguerreotype** (duh-GAIR-uh-type) to do so. They could now show what war was really like. Americans were excited by this progress. Many soldiers had their pictures taken before they went off to war.

daguerreotype camera with a picture

From Gold to Statehood

Just one month before the treaty was signed, gold was discovered! This would change the region forever. Many people moved west during the Gold Rush. They wanted to become rich. More people meant that a system of rules and laws needed to be created. Gold was valuable. It made the future state more valuable, too.

President James K. Polk wanted the rich farmland in California for the United States. In a speech to Congress in 1848, he mentioned the Gold Rush. The next year, almost 80,000 people from around the world came to the area. They wanted to get their shares of the gold. They were known as '49ers.

This map shows the two ways to go to California to find gold.

MAP OF THE GOLD REGIONS OF CALIFORNIA.
Showing the Routes via Chagres and Panama, Cape Horn, &c.

DESCRIPTION OF CALIFORNIA,

James K. Polk

A miner separates gold from rocks and dirt.

Other Golden Opportunities

Not everyone who came to California during the Gold Rush panned for gold. Many people knew the miners needed goods and services. They made or sold things the miners needed.

Economics

What to Do?

The Gold Rush drew a lot of people to California. It would not be long before the people there would ask to be a state. But two groups in Congress were focused on another key issue, which was slavery.

Abolitionists did not want slavery in the new state. Congress had an important decision to make. At the time of the Gold Rush, there were the same number of **free states** and **slave states**. If California became a state, there would be an odd number of states for one side. That worried Southerners. If slavery were not allowed in California, states in the South would lose power in Congress.

Frederick Douglass

Frederick Douglass was one of the most well-known abolitionists of his time. He was also an author. His most famous book is *Narrative of the Life of Frederick Douglass*. He wrote it in 1845. He would later argue that enslaved people should be able to fight for their freedom during the Civil War.

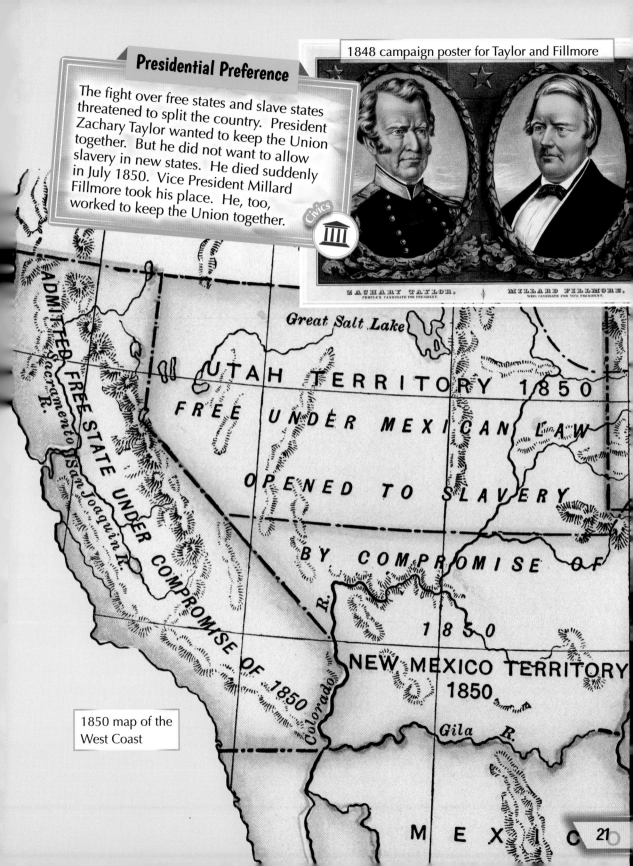

Presidential Preference

The fight over free states and slave states threatened to split the country. President Zachary Taylor wanted to keep the Union together. But he did not want to allow slavery in new states. He died suddenly in July 1850. Vice President Millard Fillmore took his place. He, too, worked to keep the Union together.

Civics

1848 campaign poster for Taylor and Fillmore

ZACHARY TAYLOR,
PEOPLE'S CANDIDATE FOR PRESIDENT.

MILLARD FILLMORE,
WHIG CANDIDATE FOR VICE PRESIDENT.

Great Salt Lake

ADMITTED FREE STATE UNDER COMPROMISE OF 1850

Sacramento R.

San Joaquin R.

UTAH TERRITORY 1850

FREE UNDER MEXICAN LAW

OPENED TO SLAVERY

BY COMPROMISE OF

1850

Colorado R.

NEW MEXICO TERRITORY 1850

Gila R.

1850 map of the West Coast

MEXICO

Compromise Pays Off

So how did Congress decide? California's future was on the line. A lot of the credit goes to Henry Clay. He was a senator from Kentucky. He came up with an agreement between the North and the South. It was called the Compromise of 1850.

This compromise wasn't just one decision. It was made up of five **bills**. First, California would be a free state. Second, there would be no more slave trading in Washington, DC. Next, enslaved people who ran away to the North would be returned to their owners in the South. This was called the Fugitive Slave Law. In the fourth bill, Texas gave up some land so the U.S. government could pay its war debt. Last, in the territories of Utah and New Mexico, it was up to the people who lived there to vote whether to allow slavery.

This was one of the most famous debates in Congress's history. And, it created the biggest state!

Clay speaks to the U.S. Senate about the Compromise of 1850.

Road to Freedom

Shadrach Minkins (SHAD-rak MIHN-kihns) was the first enslaved person arrested in the North after the Fugitive Slave Law was passed. A group of African American men in Boston stormed the courthouse where he was being held. He was **whisked** away to Canada.

The State Constitution

After Clay's compromise, there was one last step in becoming a state. California's leaders had to write a state constitution. **Delegates** met at Colton Hall in Monterey for six weeks. They created the laws for how the state would be governed.

The delegates did not have to start from scratch. They based their ideas on other constitutions. Those documents list what rights people have. And they spell out the rules for how changes can be made.

Just like the U.S. Constitution, the state government has three branches. The legislative branch makes the laws. The executive branch enforces the laws. The judicial branch interprets the laws.

The process took almost a year. On September 9, 1850, it was official. California was now the thirty-first state.

This is a re-creation of the inside of Colton Hall.

Women's Rights

Historically, women already had many rights in California. State leaders debated whether or not married women should be able to own land in California. They decided to allow women to own land. The delegates wanted women to come to the new state.

State's First Senators

William Gwin and John C. Frémont were the first U.S. senators to represent the state. They drew straws to see who would get the longer term. Frémont drew the shorter term. He ran for re-election in March 1851. He lost. He was senator for only seven months!

Changes Ahead

Being part of the United States meant changes for California. The days of being ruled by Spain and Mexico were in the past. It was much easier to govern a state with local leaders.

Interestingly, the miners created their own rules in the camps. They made specific rules around the discovery of gold. Some of these became part of the new state's laws. Miners also dealt with criminals. They helped keep law and order in the camps and nearby towns.

From Spain and missions to gold, California has a rich history. It is still changing with the times. It's exciting to think about what's next for the Golden State!

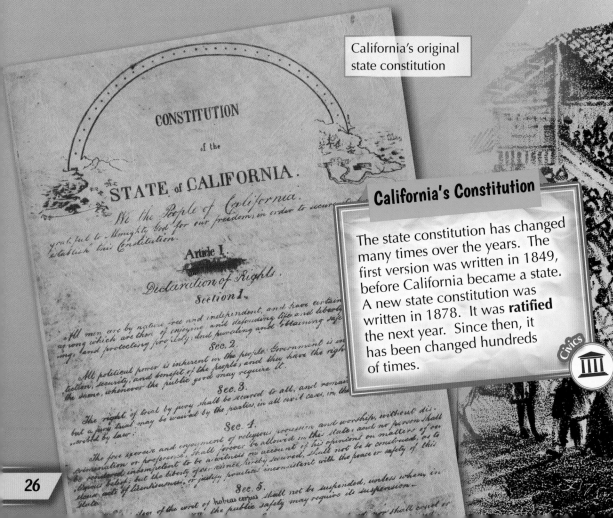

California's original state constitution

California's Constitution

The state constitution has changed many times over the years. The first version was written in 1849, before California became a state. A new state constitution was written in 1878. It was **ratified** the next year. Since then, it has been changed hundreds of times.

Civics

Ten Commandments

The discovery of gold brought some questions to light. Were there any rules? Who owned the gold? A list of rules was published in 1853. It was titled the *Miners Pioneer Ten Commandments*. These were printed and sold to miners.

The city of San Francisco celebrates California becoming a state.

Create It!

Under Mexican law, each rancho needed a brand to identify the rancho's cattle and horses. Each brand was unique. Ranchos did not have fences or backyards. Animals wandered wherever they wanted. The brand let everyone know who owned the animals.

Now, it's your turn to come up with a creative name for your rancho and design a logo. Explain the meaning behind the name and your logo. Here are some things to keep in mind. Brands usually had letters, numbers, and pictures. If an image were turned on its side, it was called "lazy." An image that was slanted was known as "tumbling."

So, for example, if your rancho were called *The Lazy Cactus*, your logo might look like this:

Glossary

abided—accepted something

abolitionists—people who were against slavery and worked to end it

annex—to add an area or region to a country or state

barred—stopped or forbade something

bills—written descriptions of new laws being proposed

Californios—wealthy ranchers who had a lot of power when California was ruled by Spain and Mexico

converted—changed from one religion or belief to another

daguerreotype—an old type of photograph made with a piece of silver

delegates—people chosen to speak for a state in making new laws and decisions about that state

free states—new states entered into the Union, which did not allow slavery

governed—ruled over and created laws for people to follow

land grants—contracts that give ownership of plots of land

ranchos—Spanish word for *ranches*; large pieces of land

ratified—made official by signing or voting

restored—returned to its original condition by repairing it and cleaning it

revolted—attempted to end someone's authority

slave states—new states entered into the Union, which allowed slavery

treaty—a formal agreement made between two or more countries or groups

whisked—moved quickly

Index

Your Turn!

CONSTITUTION
of the
STATE of CALIFORNIA.

We the People of California...

Classroom Constitution

The California Constitution sets up the rules and procedures to run the state. It is divided into sections called *articles*.

Create a classroom constitution. Use the current classroom rules or create new ones. Write at least five articles. Use language that makes the rules and procedures sound official.